ONE *with* Jesus

Spiritual Identification with Christ

One *with* Jesus

Spiritual Identification with Christ

Paul De Jaegher, S.J.

Scepter

One With Jesus is a revised edition, of the work that was last published in 1953 by The Newman Press, Westminster, Maryland

This edition is © Scepter Publishers, Inc.
First printing, 2023
info@scepterpublishers.org
www.scepterpublishers.org

Original *nihil obstat*: Edward Mahoney, S.T.D.
Original *imprimatur*: Edmund Canon Surmont, vicar general
Westminster, UK, April 29, 1929

Cover and text design: Rose Design, Inc.
Cover art: *Self-portrait with Christ* (1900), by Martin von Feuerstein (1856–1931). Courtesy: Alamy

Scripture texts from the Old and New Testaments are taken from The Holy Bible Revised Standard Version Catholic Edition © 1965 and 1966 by the Division of Christian Education of the National Council of Churches of Christ in the United States. All rights reserved. All copyrighted material is used by permission of the copyright owner. No part of it may be reproduced without permission in writing from the copyright owner.

Printed in the United States of America

ISBN: 978-159417-498-8 (pbk)
ISBN: 978-159417-499-5 (eBook)

Contents

Introduction to this Edition vii

Preface. xi

  1. Intimacy with God. 1

  2. Identification with Christ 15

  3. The Soul Identified with Jesus 25

  4. Advantages of Identification with Christ. . . 47

  5. Resolutions 65

  6. Conclusion. 71

  7. Prayer to Unite with Jesus. 77

Introduction to this Edition

THIS SHORT BOOK ATTEMPTS TO EXPLAIN and encourage the effort toward a deeper unity with our Lord Jesus Christ. Such a unity with an immaterial being may seem farfetched when viewed against all the material attractions in this world. Yet each person possesses the capability of focusing intensely on Jesus in daily life amidst any number of powerful influences. What the author provides is a guide for deepening this unity, both in the midst of, and despite, an ordinary life in the middle of the world.

The self-portrait depicted on the book cover represents how this unity with Jesus can appear. The artist, Martin von Feuerstein (1858–1931) was a German professor and a painter. He shows himself sitting at his desk, with a ghost-like, or spirit image of Jesus, who stands behind him and holds his right hand as if in blessing the painter's seated figure. It is an unusual self-portrait, in that it includes the Son of God. We can only imagine what the artist intended. But we can assume that a painter who includes someone else in a self-portrait makes a powerful statement about his relationship with that person.

This presentation of a person next to Jesus Christ is an unusual way to illustrate the point of this book. *One With Jesus, The Life of Identification with Christ*, emerged from the pen of Paul de Jaegher, S.J., (1880–1958). His purpose in writing was to explain St. Paul's doctrine of incorporation into Christ, the culmination of unity between the soul and God: "It directs the whole spiritual life towards transformation into Jesus and identification with him." (from the Preface). Rather than being satisfied with God "saving" their souls, the author praises those who generously turn themselves over to God. "God is the divine guest of my soul, dwelling there day and night, desirous of receiving the unceasing homage of my intimate friendship and of my love."

One man whose life was changed by reading de Jaegher's book was Dom Eugene Boylan, the twentieth-century author of spiritual works. Boylan discovered in de Jaegher the key to unlocking the key to the interior life, which is to seek spiritual union with Jesus Christ, the Son of God. After reading *One With Jesus*, Boylan began his own writing career, often working during the only time he had, at night, which led to his first book, *Difficulties in Mental Prayer*, and followed up with his best-known book, *This Tremendous Lover*.

As the author of *One With Jesus* drew on the 17th century French mystical writers such as Pierre Lallemant, Pierre de Berulle, and others, so did Boylan adopt the ideas from *One With Jesus* for *This Tremendous Lover*. This present edition leaves out many of the lengthy original footnotes to other works or includes explanations in the text, in order to enable the reader to follow more easily the author's flow of thought. In this slightly abridged edition, it is hoped that the author's original work can be re-presented to a new generation of readers.

Preface from the 1953 US Edition

In its ascent to God, the fervent soul generally passes through two stages. They are intimacy with Jesus and identification with him. At the beginning, the soul falls under the spell of the Master, Jesus. It is captivated by his divine lovableness and finds delight in an ever-growing intimacy with him. God often grants to the soul which has arrived at this first stage a special feeling of his divine presence which he alone can give. God thus makes this intimacy more perfect. It is a mystical grace, although many souls do not realize they are its recipients. The soul then feels as a living tabernacle, where the divine master resides and invites it into familiar conversation.

This intimacy always deepens and slowly changes itself into the second stage of identification with Jesus. The soul little by little puts aside its own feelings, to adopt those of Jesus, to let him live and act freely in that soul. This lies in deeply living for his sake and on his behalf. If the soul is generous, this process of identification is often helped by a new mystical grace.

To the feeling of his divine presence, God now adds the infused and passive feeling of his divine and transforming action. The soul feels that Christ lives in and loves it. This infused love, which penetrates, absorbs and elevates its whole being, is none other than the love for that soul which Jesus has for his own Father. The soul's life is, as it were, fused into the life of Christ within it. Now one with him, this soul's identification at every step becomes more joyful. It leads to the perfect union of sanctity, that union which is called transforming, in which the soul can cry out with the apostle Paul, "It is no longer I who live, but Christ who lives in me" (Gal 2:20).

These few pages aim at expounding a conception of the spiritual life, which, of its very nature, seems well adapted to progress through these two stages on the road to sanctity. Founded on a fundamental truth of the spiritual life, the dogma of sanctifying grace and the divine indwelling, it helps us to esteem and practice this precious intimacy with Christ, which constitutes the first stage. Then following the wonderful teaching of St. Paul on incorporation with Christ, it directs the whole spiritual life towards transformation into Jesus and identification with him. And so by continually developing in us sentiments toward the unitive life, it little by little lifts us up to the highest summits of this life.

Many souls hear little or nothing about this kind of unitive life. Few succeed in adapting their spiritual life to the consoling truths echoed by St. Paul. It is a great pity, for such souls only know the laborious side of the spiritual life and are practically unacquainted with a sweeter, purer, more affectionate side which is proper to the life of union and which identifies us with God.

By unifying love, this life of union enables us to enjoy him and his divine perfections as if they were indeed our own.

To discover this unimagined sweetness for such souls is the object of these pages.

Happy are those who delight in savoring the sublime teachings of the apostle Paul. In the garden of the Church, the divine gardener tends a thousand different blooms to charm him with their fragrance. These resemble those rare and stately orchids which, high above the flat surface of earth, find their nourishment in a cleft of rock or in the cavity of a tree, where other flowers would wither and die.

Nowadays, souls clamor for union, burning with the desire of complete offering of themselves and willing to give up the joys of their personal lives, to allow Christ, their beloved, to take that self-offering to himself. These souls are "tormented" by their unquenchable desire to love God, and sadly conscious of being unable to love or make others love him as they would wish, or as he desires.

These pages are especially for the latter but also addressed to all fervent souls. The Divine Master alone reveals to each soul in intimate conversation a deeper and more practical understanding of these truths. Such ones will know how to revel in the sublime teachings of the Apostle. The sweet after-taste of their reading will bring them back to ponder these teachings at their leisure.

It may not be out of place to remind them that mere reading, however attentive and heartfelt, can never produce lasting effects. Souls that feel themselves vibrating in unison with these thoughts must strive to taste them inwardly, to assimilate them by degrees, and by practice to reproduce them in their lives. In this way, for the pleasure of their beloved Jesus, they can exclaim with St. Paul, "For me to live is Christ, and to die is gain" (Phil 1:21).

CHAPTER ONE

Intimacy with God

IN RECENT TIMES, the doctrine of sanctifying grace and of the abiding presence of God in our souls had come close to being entirely overlooked. Now it has been brought again into the light of day. Wherever an attraction for wholesome mysticism has appeared, it has been recognized that this doctrine should be restored to the place of honor given it by the apostle St. Paul.

Although books have been published on the subject, little has been done to promote the doctrine of grace, as if it were too abstract or too difficult to understand. Many preachers and spiritual directors have developed every other subject in their sermons and instructions but avoid the topic of sanctifying grace. So those who are taught about the doctrine of grace find no more than a dry and theoretical exposition on the subject. And so their knowledge is unpractical and ineffectual. They have studied this sublime doctrine but without realizing what it means, without valuing it, and without weaving it into their lives. So, a treasure of immense value becomes regarded as something that would be better left alone.

Commune with God in our hearts

Yet it is inconceivable that such a fundamental point of religious dogma should be so discarded, and many Christians left ignorant of what might truly be called the essence of Christian life. They see only the outward appearances of that life, while its intimate and mysterious sublimity remains hidden. They live unaware of the divine adoption through sanctifying grace received in baptism, as well as other aspects such as the participation in divine nature, incorporation with Christ, priesthood of the faithful, and above all, the real presence of God in souls. They bear God within them, and do not even know it. All these wonders of Pauline doctrine are utterly unknown to them.

Is it not sad to see the benefits of a loving God so little appreciated and even entirely unsuspected?

God's ecstatic love reveals itself especially in a twofold gift: on the one hand, the Incarnation and Holy Eucharist, and on the other, the presence of God in the sanctified and deified soul. The first gift, which is a physical manifestation, is well known. The second, which is spiritual, can for many seem non-existent. And who is responsible for this? Those who should have understood, delighted in, and by their lives expressed these truths, and then strived with enthusiasm to make them known.

Now, much has been lost to the spiritual life by this neglect. What elation beyond the trivialities of this life would come from awareness that we are no longer simply children of men, but sons and daughters of God. How contemptible would appear mere earthly things, considering that we are naturalized children of God, and so we become transformed into his being. Above all, how it would transform the lives of Christians were they only to realize this sublime truth: God is the divine guest of my soul, dwelling there day and night, desirous of receiving the unceasing homage of my intimate friendship and my love.

What greater incentive to the practice of the interior life and recollection if we incorporate these considerations into our lives. In comparison, how weak and ineffectual are the many other motives so often proposed, such as praise for a recollected life, the dangers of dissipation, perhaps even an occasional mention that God is everywhere present, hearing our most secret thoughts. Unspoken is the knowledge that God stands in need of our friendship, and to obtain it, gives himself intimately to us and makes us his "heaven," his living tabernacles. Not emphasized is it that, though we cannot always accompany the God-Man on our altars, we can like St. Catherine of Siena withdraw ourselves to commune with the God in our hearts. No consideration more than this one enables a life of unceasing prayer and continuous conversation with God.

Is not the love of interior recollection and familiar discourse with God a special characteristic of interior souls? If they have great devotion to Jesus in the Blessed Sacrament, they are equally devoted to Jesus the Eternal Word, the guest and life of their soul. But it is regrettable that, on account of the silence maintained on the dogma of the Abiding Presence within us, many souls take so long to attain to this practice of devotion to God as their heart's guest, while others never reach it in all their spiritual life.

The doctrine of grace, and especially a firmly implanted belief in the presence of God within us, may have a great influence on the development of mystic life and passive prayer. The very term "passive" proves that it is a pure gift of God. Although the soul may to a great extent prepare itself for the reception of this treasure, God does not plant his divine seed where he sees it is endangered from being choked off by selfish and worldly desires. As a consequence we can and ought to prepare ourselves for the reception and development of this divine gift by removing obstacles to it.

According to St. John of the Cross, the chief characteristic of mystical prayer is an indefinable loving remembrance of God—vague, indistinct, and passively experienced. This prince of mystical theology speaks of it incessantly, as he described in *The Ascent of Mount Carmel* and *The Dark Night of the Soul*. He declares in no uncertain terms that we must in no way desire ecstasies and other extraordinary favors, yet we cannot too highly esteem or too earnestly desire and ask for this loving union with God which forms the very essence of the mystic union. Hence we can see no better preparation for passive prayer than a habitual loving and active attention to the divine guest of our heart.

A vast gulf lies between this active, loving attention and the passive and infused one, and God alone can bridge the abyss. None the less, a close relationship exists between the two. The soul, which delights in communing with its divine guest, experiences sentiments that are harmonious with those of supernatural prayer. These sentiments prepare the soul for that prayer, and in a way invite the soul into that prayer. We can reasonably think that God's goodness, at seeing the soul so disposed and attentive, will not be outdone in generosity by leaving the soul to carry on this loving conversation alone. Occasionally, and by degrees more frequently, God enables the soul to hear that divine response which when received passively, is mystic prayer. Thus, while the soul is insensible under the divine action, its attention becomes the loving passive and infused attention of supernatural prayer.

Eliminating obstacles

So far, we have examined the positive element of preparation. The negative element consists in eliminating obstacles. To name only one, the chief obstacle to the mystical life is the lack of recollection, and its associated state, dissipation of mind and heart.

The great teachers of prayer, St. Teresa of Avila and St. John of the Cross, insisted on the mind and heart being emptied of created things. Thus memory, understanding and will must be purged, and then strictly controlled. Their natural inclinations must be directed toward a constant and loving turning towards God. A soul that is penetrated with the great reality of God's presence seeks instinctively to unify its aims and tend wholly to God. Mindful of the precious jewel it guards within, it turns to God unceasingly in thoughts and affections. All its powers are concentrated on God, who like a magnet draws the soul towards him. The soul's perfections grow in their attraction to God, while created things fade more and more into insignificance and gradually into oblivion. Distracting influences tend to disappear and cease to trouble the soul in the exercise of this loving attention which God wishes to impart through mystic prayer. God aids its long purification to become still more simple and more spiritual. The painful "night of the senses" envelops the soul to bring about in its depths what that soul by its own efforts cannot accomplish.

Through such a trial, God detaches the soul from all outward things and brings about the passive purification of the senses. The soul during this period suffers great aridity and, in spite of its fervor, which is real, although not sensible, is convinced of its own lukewarmness. Furthermore, the soul in that state becomes incapable of following a definite method in meditation as it formerly did. The process underway is the secret transition from meditation to inward and mystic contemplation.

Far beyond sense purifications, the advantages of devotion to the three divine Persons are just beginning. Once the soul passes through its purification, it crosses the threshold of mystic prayer. Now, even in the earlier stages of infused contemplation, the soul often experiences a distinct passive sense of the divine presence, which is a gratuitous gift of God. God makes himself felt experimentally and passively, and draws the soul to himself.

Some see in this infused sense of the divine presence an essential and characteristic note of all mystic prayer. This seems hard to accept, for one needs to acknowledge that the infused loving concentration of the mind on God must not be confused with the infused sense of his presence. It can even be very well connected to the sorrowful feeling of God's absence, as is often the case of the trials of the "dark night of the soul." Without going so far, this feeling is in practice a sign which indicates the presence of supernatural prayer. It can be certain that at the outset of the time of transition, many are conscious of their entrance in the mystical life through their passive sense of the divine presence.

Hence, it is easy to see how useful it can be to inculcate the devotion to the divine presence within us. Too many souls regard it merely as a metaphor. This is regrettable, for the time comes unexpectedly when God invites them to withdraw into themselves in order to converse with him in the prayer of passive recollection or quiet. He will give them that exquisite sense of his divine presence, although in a very faint degree at the outset. But unfortunately, if the soul is ignorant of the reality of this presence, and accustomed only to see God as outside of it, then the soul probably takes no heed. Unaware of the grace offered to it, the soul runs the risk of not hearing the divine invitation, or at least of not appreciating its full value. After enjoying a time of divine intimacy, it perhaps becomes dissipated. Once more it seeks creature comforts, thus rendering itself unworthy of further favors.

Impact of the abiding presence

Now consider a soul which has for a long time lived the doctrine of the abiding presence. Accustomed by its own effort and helped by grace, it converses affectionately and simply with its beloved. It acquires a real devotion to the soul's guest, as well as to the dweller in the tabernacle. This soul instantaneously feels the mystic touches, however delicate they may be. It thrills with joy at the slightest passive experience of

God's presence. How great its happiness now, for not only does it know, but tastes with delight, the presence of the beloved one. Full of gratitude and love for this great good, it henceforth concentrates all efforts on making itself worthy of new favors.

None deny that many souls never attain to mystic prayer, and that many never advance, through lack of sound spiritual teaching. The Mexican mystic, Miguel Godinez (1591–1644) estimated that 90 percent of souls called to passive prayer were hindered by the lack of good direction. If this seems to be an exaggerated claim, it was reinforced by St. John of the Cross who criticized those who only sought to teach the discursive method of prayer, in which they digress from one subject to another, rather than concentrate on God alone.

Many others, without being a positive hindrance, do not sufficiently help those they guide toward infused contemplation. Were they more deeply imbued with the sense of divine presence in the soul, they would better understand the repugnance for discursive prayer felt by those who have arrived on the threshold of the mystical life. They would allow these souls to devote a part of the time allotted to prayer, or even all of it, to paying a loving attention to the God present within them and making what has been rightly called the prayer of simple presence. Their duty as directors of other souls would then be to study the subject more thoroughly, to live what they have learned, and to strive to instill into others those great truths of faith which form the basis of the mystic life. In this way, without being aware of it, they would direct many toward passive prayer. Thus, by inspiring the sentiments which would prepare them for passive prayer, they dispose them more favorably to receive it.

What applies to the beginning of mystic prayer is equally true for its further development. All mystic souls naturally tend to seek their God within themselves. Even if their understanding of the doctrine of sanctifying grace leads them to think that the life of God within us is only metaphorical, nevertheless they sense that God is in their soul, at least occasionally. St. Francis de Sales observed that bees return to the hive because of the sweetness of the honey; thus the mystic soul loves to seek God within itself, knowing by experience how pleasant is his company.

How many would apply themselves to intimate communion with God with more care and perseverance, if they were instructed, and if they realized that God present within them regrets how that soul wastes itself on exterior, earthly things. St. Teresa of Avila in her autobiography describes her joy in hearing from a spiritual director that God, whose presence within her she often felt, was in very truth continually present in the soul by sanctifying grace. In *The Interior Castle*, she fixated on the abiding presence of God in the soul. This illustrious contemplative often complained that many souls given to prayer seek God very far from them in a distant heaven, instead of seeking and easily finding him in their own hearts.

CHAPTER TWO

Identification with Christ

From the consideration so far of God's special presence in the soul from sanctifying grace, it's time to turn to other dynamic elements which also invigorate the soul. God is present within us, not only as a divine guest who comes to receive our adoration and love, but more especially to die to self and to live in him, to transform and make us God-like. The divine life which began at baptism should develop and grow unceasingly until the day when it reaches its end in heaven.

Here we see at once the heart of St. Paul's marvelous doctrine, the principal work of his apostolate in his epistles: "For you have died, and your life is hid with Christ in God" (Col 3:3). By baptism we die to a natural life, but in dying with him (*commortui*, buried with him (*consepulti*), rising with him (*conresuscitati*), we are born again as children of God. Christ is within us. "*Induimini Christum*"—Put on Jesus Christ. "For as many of you as were baptized into Christ have put on Christ" (Gal 3:27). At every opportunity, Paul speaks of this life. "For if we have been united with him in a death like his, we shall certainly be united with him in a resurrection like his. "(Rom 6:5). We recall in particular his celebrated comparison of the body's head and members: "For just as the body is one and has many members, and all the members of the body, though many, are one body, so it is with Christ. . . . Now you are the body of Christ, and individually members of it." (1 Cor 12: 12, 27).

The doctrine of God's life with us and our incorporation with Christ is so fruitful for the soul's life that it may be examined from many viewpoints. Which aspect we choose will lead us to form a different conception of the spiritual life, but each will have something in common with the others, merely showing shades of difference in details. The emphasis should be on considering what is best suited to lead us to the heights of the unitive life.

Love for his Father prompted Christ to become Man. His thirty-three years on earth were wholly consecrated to this love and to seeking his father's glory. He lived a drama of divine love, the greatest suffering of which was shown in his death on Calvary. But Christ is risen. Although he died he still lives. The immense love of the God-Man did not end with the grave. Its influence extends beyond the narrow confines of Jesus's human life.

Jesus's love for his Father

The glorified Jesus still experiences Golgotha. What does this mean? That Jesus will be content to love his father infinitely in heaven, and in each of our tabernacles? Not so. Great as this love would be, it doesn't satisfy the heart of Christ. He desires more. The drama of Jesus's love for his father continues here on earth. For Jesus, by his life and redemption, made for himself a mystical body. He continues to live in it, to love and to glory his father. To love the more, he unites himself to new individual human natures, to billions of them, in a very real, intimate, and wonderful way. The completed love of Christ is the love of his heart, united to countless millions of Christians who will love with him and in him to the end of time. The is the great masterpiece that divine love accomplishes. This alone succeeds in quenching the infinite love-thirst which Christ has for his Father.

Jesus then is forever yearning to love his Father with extravagant abandon. He yearns to love the Father not only by his own divine life, nor only with his heart on fire with love, but in millions of hearts and lives to the end of time.

His infinite love needs to express itself, to pour itself out in an infinity of ways. What then does Jesus wish? He wants hearts that will give themselves up to him, to abandon themselves completely to him, to allow him to satisfy freely, in them and by them, his infinite passion of divine love. To enter a closer union with each of his members, he asks for the entire possession of their being, body, and soul, that he may make them his own, to take them over and live through them his devotion to his beloved Father.

What Jesus Wants

The thirty-three years of Jesus's earthly life were not enough. The unquenchable passion of his love would forever continue in love, work, prayer, and suffering. In the expression of Sister Elizabeth of the Trinity, he seeks from each of us another human life. He says: Give me your heart, that in you and through you, in a life of union I may love, or rather *we* may love the father ardently. Give me your lips so that together we may sing his praises. Give me your mind, your eyes, your hands, your whole being. I wish through you to live as it were a second life completely of love. It will be the complement and continuation of my earthly life at Nazareth and in Palestine.

How completely sublime then, is the Christian life, sublimity undreamt by so many souls. How ardent are the desires of Jesus's heart, too little known even to generous souls! The Christian is not only his or her own person, nor a mere human personality, but something of Jesus, a way of Jesus himself, divinized through incorporation with Christ. Each one lives not merely a petty personal life with its restricted horizon. It has a much deeper significance. It is, and must be, before all and above all the life of Christ within us, the continuation of Jesus's life. Such a magnificent ideal is well calculated to transform and render our whole life sublime.

How do we realize it? In every action we perform, every prayer we say, every suffering we endure, in every act of love we must bear in mind that we are "Christ." This Christ wishes still to act, pray, suffer and love in us. We then set aside our unrestrained, miserly, limited desires, in order to absorb the wider understanding and the unlimited desires which animated Jesus in his actions, prayers and sufferings during his earthly life.

We must surrender ourselves to Christ so completely as to become only his instrument; to give him absolute freedom of action in us, all but losing our personality in our complete abandonment. We must live only on his behalf and in his name, to see all from his point of view, and thus to surrender ourselves wholly to him so that we live and grow without hindrance until our life be one with his. This is the ideal and the height of spirituality that should be better known: the ideal and spirituality of St. Paul, of whom it was said: "*Cor Pauli, Cor Christi*"—The heart of Paul is the heart of Christ.

Offering ourselves to Christ

Now an important distinction arises. We run the risk of considerably minimizing the sublime ideal just mentioned if we think it means that we offer ourselves to Christ so that he descends to our own level and lives *our* life, and not *his* life, within us. At the outset, these two aspects seem much alike. However, the latter is infinitely superior to the former. Just a moment's thought makes the difference clear.

In the first aspect, the soul that wishes to identify with Christ does not invite Jesus to come down by adapting itself to its views and aspirations. It does not ask Jesus to unite himself to the soul, only for the sake of a more pure and holy life. It does not content itself with praying, suffering and loving, as before, although with more intensity and purity of purpose. Such action would appear very noble but insufficient.

In the second aspect, *his* life in *us*, the soul thinks, loves and prays differently. It asks Christ to live his life in the soul, and for his sake. It wants Jesus to continue his own life within it, not to begin in it a new life, which although holy perhaps, would be restricted by a creature's limited vision. The soul now stripped of self makes room for Christ; Jesus then lives his own life there. The heart of Christ beats in its breast. It makes its own, all Jesus's interests, views, loves and desires, which are as far-reaching as the universe, and perfectly free from all self-love.

This union not only helps the soul become better, and to purify and find itself. It helps the soul to forsake itself once and for all, to renounce its own perspective for that of Jesus.

Some may consider this approach too fanciful, a hint of quietism, which is the acceptance of everything without any resistance or effort to change them. Or it may be considered too sublime, and too impersonal, to be attractive to more than a few. Although this aspect of the spiritual life is lofty and it demands a great and continual self-denial, the soul will often fail to follow it. Unawares, it falls frequently back on itself, and while thinking that it allows Christ to expand his life within it, it only unites itself to Christ to be more holy.

Instead of the great heart of Jesus with its boundless desires, its own poor heart still animates its spiritual life. The soul unconsciously lives, not on the superior plane with Jesus, but on its own inferior one. These two lives will cross each other, and frequently intermingle. If the soul is faithful in rising again each time to the higher plane, if it does not stop looking up to its ideal, and strives always to substitute Jesus for self, it will someday attain the long-for heights. It will require perhaps quite special graces, but one thing is sure: It will finally acquire that life more divine than human, the commencement of the heavenly life, the life of Christ within it. The soul will fully realize the words of St. Paul: "It is no longer I who live, but Christ who lives in me" (Gal 2:20).

CHAPTER THREE

The Soul Identified with Jesus

THE FEATURES OF A SOUL that allows Jesus to live in it deserve more of a sketch than an explanation. To begin with, this sketch does more than lengthy reasoning to illustrate this soul's profile.

Such a soul no longer prays for its own sake as it did formerly; its prayer is not its alone. Rather, it is the prayer of Jesus, one might even say *only* that of Jesus. It knows that it does not pray alone, but that its most-beloved prays with it.

With what joy it now says "Our Father, who art in heaven." God is the father of Jesus and its own father. Assisted by Jesus within, this soul instinctively and gradually reproduces the prayer of Jesus on the mountain. In forgetting itself, it discards its narrow interests and small-mindedness of the past, and its prayer expands beyond measure. When it adores, its action is no longer the offering of its own self, but instead the immense worship which Jesus offers within it. This action is in Jesus own name, and on behalf of the whole mystical body.

In Jesus and with Jesus it incessantly gives thanks, not so much for benefits received from God, but for those which God has lavished on Jesus and on all his mystical members. Above all, it loves God passionately for the Jesus's sake and in Jesus's name. It also loves him for those countless millions of men and women who alas love him so little.

Freedom from self-concern

This soul living in Jesus's name no longer bends under the weight of its own thoughts, where "I" am the center of prayer. Even more, it no longer concentrates on the correction of faults and failings, nor does the prayer consist in begging for graces for itself and others. Happiness now means to contemplate and to enjoy the infinite perfections of God or his son, Jesus. The soul now loves to "lose itself," to forget itself by turning towards God in loving contemplation and admiration of the divine perfections, as Jesus himself did in his prayer to the father during his earthly life. Thus, the divine perfections of Jesus now constitute the soul's wealth, treasure, and happiness.

Its prayer to the Blessed Virgin Mary is similarly changed, for here again, Jesus prays through the soul. The soul feels it unmistakably and cannot forget it. Jesus therefore gives the soul a child's love. And Mary returns these caresses as she did those of her Christ child. Mary makes herself so sweet, so delightful, so charming and so intimate, that at times the soul soars with joy, for Mary now so appears to be its true mother. In the past, Mary meant nothing, but now she assumes the role of a mother in that soul's regard.

These are a few of the main qualities of such a soul's prayer. But its prayer is not limited to specific times set aside for formal conversation with God. The whole day gradually becomes an uninterrupted prayer. When fully conscious of Jesus's presence and of his action in its soul, it cannot fail to remember him. Repulsed by all its personal interests and living solely for Jesus and in him, it becomes impossible not to live continually, or nearly so, for Jesus's sake. In the passion of its love, it seems that not to live *with* Jesus means not to live *for* him. His companionship alone gives charm and interest to all the soul's actions. In the eager desire to please him, it does not lose sight of him for any length of time.

Depth of intimacy

Who then can express the depth and tenderness of intimacy with Jesus? The soul does everything for its lover. Each action takes place hand in hand with him. It is likely that Jesus powerfully helps the soul that is so close to him to keep alive his divine presence. He makes the soul ascend step by step the degrees of mystical life and prayer and bestows the precious gift of an "active quiet" that is ever increasing and habitual. Soon the most distracting activities cease to absorb such a soul. In its inner heart it always unites with the master until it hardly perceives any difference between prayer time and work or recreation. This mystic prayer of quiet is prolonged beyond the time of prayer and possesses the soul amid active work.

It is not with Jesus only that the soul dwells and communes. United to him and in his name, it speaks constantly to the Father and the Holy Spirit. Some, like St. Elizabeth of the Trinity, in union with Jesus, adored and loved the Trinity in a particular way within themselves. Others, while communing with Jesus in their souls, were more inclined to converse in his name and for him, with God, whom they felt present near and around them, and in whom they felt as if drowned in an ocean of love. It would be interesting to study in this connection the different mentalities of souls. Many influences serve to draw them towards their particular form of devotion, but they are mainly attracted by the nature of the mystic graces they have received. The presence of God can show itself more clearly near them than in them, or vice versa.

This presence of God arises without any words. It is like a loving glance, a silent turning of the soul and of Jesus towards God. Silent as it is, it is yet most eloquent. At each hour it offers to the Father its actions, prayers, sufferings, loving aspirations and desires which Jesus produces, and which are so many expressions of its love for God. Inadequate as they are, and spoiled by the instrument's imperfection, the soul still knows that God accepts them. Therefore, the soul seeks something better to offer, namely itself in union with the heart of Jesus, who is the soul's source of love. It offers back to God his purity, his unbounded devotion, his unfathomable humility, and all his infinite perfections.

It first offers them to the Father, to satisfy the burning desires of Jesus and then to repair and in a manner, to drown with these desires the sins of the whole world. Above all, the soul delights in offering to God the love of Jesus dying on the Cross, when in a supreme act of sacrifice he gave sublime expression to the love of his divine heart. With what emotion and loving confidence, the soul says to the Father: "Behold my Jesus dying for you. Does his unbounded love not satisfy your desires? I see how he pleads for the world's salvation. Can you reject his love and refuse to answer his prayer?"

In summary, the day of the soul identified with Jesus is more than a continual prayer. It is an offering like a continual Mass. Each day's holy sacrifice is only the culminating point and most solemn moment of that continual sacrifice.

In this way, love is bound to increase continually in the soul. Love permeates its whole life. No longer will love be feeble, restricted, and mixed with self-seeking, as in the past when it loved God but also managed to love itself in some way separate from God. How could Jesus permit such love, or give expression to it through the soul, when he sees and loves in all things none but his heavenly Father? Jesus could not live in a soul so tainted with self-interested love. Therefore, he inflames the soul with his own love. He makes the soul see everything in the light of his radiant love. And now, loving with the love of Jesus, the soul hates its loathsome self, and setting its face against this theft, wings its flight towards God. Like Jesus, and for his sake, the soul loves God, and God alone. All the rest disappears. The Blessed Virgin Mary, the saints, the whole world, only manifest and reflect the vision of divine lovableness. The soul sees God in every creature.

More astonishing than all else, the soul would never dream that its love has become so pure that in loving itself, it is God whom it sees and loves. Animated and vivified by Jesus, and loving only through him, it flees from the slightest self-complacency in thinking about itself, which was once the object of its affections. God is now its entire object, and as it discerns him in all things, it loses itself in outpourings of love. It reaches the fourth and last degree of love mentioned by St. Bernard of Clairvaux, which consists in loving God alone.

Jesus loves in the soul; henceforth the soul will love God, not only as its *only* good, but as its *own* good, its very own possession. This is the true love of union, the love with which Jesus loves his Father. The soul knows that God is its possession. Jesus gives himself to a soul that gives itself to him. The soul can then say, "*Deus meus et omnia*"—"O my God, you are all mine, my very own." And this cry fills it with rapturous joy and love. It throws off its beggar rags, which are the semblance of virtue which once filled the soul with secret complacency. It will never look at them again. The soul becomes a queen, and the king's treasures belong to it. The soul loves as its own, as something personal, the attractions and infinite perfections of God and Jesus, its beloved. Jesus in turn says, "Forsake all your false treasures of former days, abandon yourself above all, and I will give myself to you. All that is mine is yours. Love it as your own possession."

Christ accomplishes this exchange through the immensity of his love. And the soul, in response to such an outpouring, loses itself in wonder. In former days it lost itself in loving its ugly self. Now it melts away with love, at the sight of the infinite lovableness that attracts and ravishes.

As a result, knowing one's natural imperfections and failings no longer causes distress. In the past it dreamed of throwing off those miseries and by degrees replacing them with a beauty of its own creation, in which it could draw a secret complacency. Instead of this imperfect beauty for which it yearned, God gives it his own beauty, which fills it with paroxysms of love.

Life of Abandonment

True love is gift of self. We love to the extent we give ourselves to another. We love fully only when we give ourselves without reserve. On this basis, the summit of love is the life of abandonment. And in what does this life consist, which is superior to the love of suffering, and more exalted than any other form of spirituality: in the definite and complete surrender of self, inspired by an ardent love. The soul surrenders unreservedly to its beloved, to be possessed. Is not this exactly what a soul does, whose ever-present ideal is to identify with Jesus to unite in closest union with him? Its whole life consists in abandonment to Jesus. It would not consciously entertain a single desire, fear, or regret which is not inspired by Jesus.

All its desires now tend to self-annihilation, understood as the substitution of Jesus for oneself. Each instant repeats the being's immolation, each action is a pouring forth, a blending of its life with that of its divine friend. At each moment the will meets and embraces the will of Jesus, and in this perpetual embrace its life flows onwards, producing a truly sublime existence and a prelude to what awaits it in heaven.

Happy soul, to have thus escaped. It has reached what has been so aptly called the "spiritual" ecstasy. What does it matter whether it be favored with corporal delight: it is quite ready for the final transformation into Jesus, the sign indicating a "transforming union."

The soul reaches the summit of love. It is irrevocably, and violently in love with God, and can only be satisfied by meeting him face-to-face in heaven. St. Paul uses the phrase "*Caritas Christi urget nos.*" "For the love of Christ controls (urges) us . . ." (2 Cor 5:14). The love of Christ for his father invades the heart and penetrates its being. "You have ravished my heart" (Song 4:9). The divine perfections, of which the soul has an occasional glimpse, leave an unhealed wound on the heart. Forever will the soul love the infinitely loveable God to the full extent of its desires. Its love will be both its Calvary and its Tabor, its greatest suffering, and its most exquisite enjoyment. Worn out by the fever of love, it cries out with St. Teresa, "*Muero porque no muero.*" (I die because I cannot die).

Who can describe the humility of a soul that lives in Jesus's name? What is true humility, but the love of God even at the price of contempt of self? Does not such a soul, each day, ardently desire nothing except that Jesus completely possesses it? From the day it resolves to substitute Jesus for self, to identify itself with Jesus, it knows no other goal. To be nothing and to count for nothing, fills it with an intense delight that is entirely unknown to others.

Humility of heart

Such a soul learns the secret of true "lowliness of heart." Each new disclosure of its inherent wretchedness and imperfection, instead of troubling it, brings joy. It loves and gives thanks for these miseries permitted by God. After all, does not its depth of poverty highlight, by contrast, God's infinite love? Does God not find recompense in this way for all the glory formerly denied him, by the soul's vanity or secret self-complacency? Does not the soul's happiness really consist in seeing that God is all, and all else is nothing? That, out of God, everything created is merely dust? What could only disturb the soul would be to hear that God is not all, that besides him something else stands, no matter how small or insignificant. But it knows this cannot be. The soul's joy and glory consist in realizing that God the Infinite triumphs over all, Being and Goodness over nothingness and evil.

It renounces its own glory and enriches itself infinitely, since it regards as its own the glory of the Most High. The glory of the Trinity, which is given to God by our Savior Jesus and innumerable legions of angels and saints, now makes up the soul's glory. This becomes its pride, and in this alone does it find a secret complacency. In contrast, any praise from others seems a mockery.

Appearing to be humble, no one realizes the soul's wretchedness and poverty. Its overarching desire is to let Jesus pervade, so that what comes forth is his humility, charity and forgetfulness of self. Nonetheless, the soul still sometimes falls short of its goal. Oftentimes the ego rises up and takes the place of Jesus. Despite these occurrences, an ever-present consciousness of Jesus dwelling within reveals these attempts of the natural and selfish life to recover its dominance. This consciousness of Jesus gives an intuition of whatever is not right, whatever "is not Jesus," and could not be Jesus.

Immediately recognized is a passing feeling of vanity, an almost imperceptible impulse toward self-seeking, or a slight and merely physical movement of impatience. With any effort of self-examination, the soul perceives at once that such a thought or movement could never proceed from Christ living within. Both life and breath must be "Christ" purely and simply. "For to me to live is Christ, and to die is gain" (Phil 1:21). The soul, knowing that Jesus uses it to glory his father and that it should be a continual hymn which sings to God. Unfortunately, it introduces many discordant notes into what should be a perfect song of praise.

Hope never fails

Though conscious of its extreme poverty, the soul still trusts implicitly its heavenly Father, or because it feels so poor and miserable that it trusts even more in God. Having long lost faith in its own powers, it no longer trusts in its virtues, which were the chief obstacle to a pure trust in God. Expecting nothing from itself, but everything from God, it experiences his infinite goodness that is so different from its earthly variety. God's goodness lovingly condescends to what is most vile and poor.

Its hope never fails because it is never alone. Nor does it go alone to the heavenly father, because it always accompanies Christ, his beloved son. He is the guarantee of being welcomed and affectionately embraced, a poor beggar in rags. What difference would that make? The humble soul can approach the king of heaven with unbounded confidence by presenting the infinite merits of Jesus. It confidently offers the virtues of his son, and takes care to conceal the defects of its own virtues. Above all the gifts offered is the heart of Jesus, through which the desire to love the Father is satisfied with a boundless love.

In this love, anything desired of God is sure of being heard. "If you ask anything of the Father in my name, he will give it to you. Hitherto, you have asked nothing in my name; ask and you will receive, that your joy may be full" (Jn 16:23–24). Why would you fail to receive since it is Jesus himself, who entreats his Father on your behalf? To refuse the request would be to refuse his son. The soul no longer deserves, as many do, the reproach of Jesus for not asking, nor does it know to ask of God except in Jesus. For a long time, its prayers and its very life have been in the name of Christ.

Take note of the nobility and greatness of the soul who identifies with Christ. How greatly its life is expanded and ennobled. From the day it began to live for Jesus, new and widening horizons open out before it. Like a glow-worm that was accustomed to see only a narrow range illumined by its tiny light, it now lives in the brightness of the sun, with a wider vision.

A new world unfolds itself, all radiant with heavenly light. By seeing with the savior's point of view, the soul's petty and selfish interests become transformed into the desires of Jesus. Its love embraces the whole world. Wherever the life of Jesus pulsates, its influence is felt. It knows that through him, it can sanctify the remotest parts of the earth. United to Jesus and to his entire mystical body, the soul possesses not one heart, but millions, which it wants to set throbbing with divine love. It possesses millions of lives which Jesus transforms. It exults at the thought that it can multiply a thousandfold, to love God in thousands of hearts, and in this way satisfy its own thirst for love. At the same time, it suffers. With St. Paul it cries out, "My little children, with whom I am again in travail until Christ be formed in you!" (Gal 4:19).

What need is there to emphasize the happiness of a soul entirely devoted to Jesus and living in his name? Like a prisoner set free, the soul was once the captive of too personal a life, shut up within a narrow, subjective spirituality. Freed from captivity, the heart expands with a strong, joyful beat. The greatness of this life is immeasurable, as it is the life of Jesus himself. The breadth of the soul's life is now to please God, to rejoice in the heavenly Father. A joy of this nature never fails. Despite any miseries, it can always, through Jesus, please the God whom it loves.

Another Joy

An infinitely refined joy that is too little known arises from hatred and contempt of oneself. It is known only to the initiated, to those who are in love with God. The soul which is perfectly united to Jesus is familiar with it. Souls so enamored with the perfections of God the Father easily recognize the ugly and contemptible, which by contrast with God enhances his attraction. In its passionate love for God, it rejoices at seeing itself so unlovely and defective. What causes grief to mediocre and self-centered souls is to her a source of secret joy.

But the essential and fundamental happiness of such a soul must be sought higher still—in God himself. The love of Jesus intimately unites the soul to God. God fills the heart in the place of the self. He becomes the other self. God's infinite perfections constitute the soul's own happiness. This joy experienced by saints becomes the soul's purest happiness and the soul sees it in every creature. From this fountain of God's bliss, the soul drinks deep draughts of joy, above all in the beauties of nature. Each flower, each blade of grass, each insect, says to it: "See how beautiful God is! How great and happy!"

Even more, this supreme ecstasy of the soul is unchangeable like the happiness of God himself. Nothing can disturb its peace and joy, for they are secure in the serenity of the divine perfections. Since the soul's happiness is identified with God, it is unchangeably happy because God is infinitely so.

The soul may suffer and suffer much. It may pine away on a bed of suffering, and see displayed its own shortcomings or the triumph of vice. Nothing ripples the surface of its deep lake of happiness.

CHAPTER FOUR

Advantages of Identification with Christ

IN THE OUTLINE SO FAR SKETCHED of the soul, the outstanding feature is the unitive life that is stamped on all its virtues. From its former efforts at improvement, it now aspires to the conscious understanding that the soul is one with Jesus, that it possesses what belongs to Jesus, and that it possesses his perfections. Jesus infuses into the soul his unitive love. The soul loves with Jesus's love, and all the soul's virtues feel the happy effect of his love.

Prayer now consists in lovingly contemplating and delighting in the divine perfections. Not satisfied with loving God *alone*, the soul loves him as its own. Since it takes a loving delight in

God, its happiness consists less in serving and pleasing God, than in enjoying the happiness of God himself. Everything in life and in nature gives joy because everything speaks of the divine greatness, beauty, wisdom, and happiness. The soul's humility is also a form of unitive love. It gladly despises itself, and counts itself as nothing, because God is everything.

All such sentiments characterize the unitive life. Since these sentiments are newly felt, this novelty startles those who are taking their first steps on the spiritual way of identification with Jesus Christ. After only a few months, in some cases, life seems to be completely changed. They have the impression of being immersed and overwhelmed in the sublime, in the same way that an alpine climber reaching a summit marvels at the magnificent panorama of peaks, glaciers and valleys spread out in all directions.

This sense of a bold, new vision results from the unitive nature of the spiritual way. Up to the present the soul never learned to rejoice with Jesus at the infinite happiness of God, or of the

Blessed Virgin, to find consolation for sufferings, as well as faults and imperfections, in the thought that it counts for little: "God is happy, God is God; this is happiness enough for me." No one ever suggested that it seek happiness in the perpetual homage which the persons of the Blessed Trinity render each other. Nor to rejoice at the Father's perfections, as if they were its own, or to be lifted with joy at the thought that God the Father is infinitely loved by Jesus and Jesus by him, or to thank Jesus for his great love for his Father and his Blessed Mother, and finally, the happiness of God in nature, which reminds us of him.

Very seldom do these considerations come up in books of meditation, and even then only briefly outlined. The thoughts and affections normally relate to the purgative and illuminative ways of holiness and are usually directed to the correction of a fault or acquisition of a virtue. Rather than being centered on the soul, or self-centered, they should be more Christ-centered, or God-centered. How much the soul would gain, to try to see itself from God's point of view.

Not only does a spiritual life of assimilation to Christ favor the growth of sentiments harmonious to the unitive life, but it gives the soul a sure path. Initially, the soul renounces a self-centered life to live Christ's life. According to such as St. Thomas Aquinas, St. Teresa and St. John of the Cross, the soul takes root in the unitive life when its will is no longer separate from the Lord's. The soul's union with God supposes the blend of two wills into one. From this point, the soul no longer considers, at least voluntarily, any personal or selfish feelings of joy, regret, fear, or hope. It admits nothing but the thoughts and desires of God.

What is the essence of this life of identification with Christ if not the absolute stripping of the soul to clothe itself with Jesus Christ? From the beginning, it directs itself to this end: to diminish, to die, to be nothing any longer, so that Christ may be everything. "He must increase, but I must decrease" (Jn 3:30). The soul desires with all its strength, thoughts and affections to renounce all self-will so that it wants only what Christ wills. It knows it is Christ in the making, and that in its case sanctity consists in making ever more and more room for Christ, until, like the host in the tabernacle, it retains human appearances, but is interiorly divine and wholly identified with Jesus and transformed into him.

This conception of the spiritual life has still other advantages.

First, its marvelous simplicity. It would be impossible to find a more simplified form of spirituality. The soul's whole program is condensed and concentrated into one leading idea which is also a magnificent ideal: to renounce yourself in order to allow Christ to do all things in you. This idea encompasses all the virtues, a practice even more perfect if motivated by love for each act of virtue. The soul needs no lengthy reasoning to live patience, humility, charity or self-forgetfulness. It is enough to be faithful to the desire for Christ to produce these and other virtues. Enough motivation lies in the consciousness or memory of his presence.

Ab extra, ab intra

Formerly, the soul's spirituality was more complicated. It loved commentaries on the virtues or the vices. Or the soul encouraged itself in the practice of virtues by an imitation of Jesus, a kind of imitation *ab extra*, from outside. Jesus was a model, but outside of it, whose virtues the soul tried to reproduce after the fashion of a painter who copies his subject. But now Jesus means something very different. To imitate Jesus no longer means to copy him, but to be transformed into him. It is to allow Christ to develop and reproduce himself in it. It is imitation *ab intra*, from within.

It is not a question of becoming merely like Jesus, but of being one with Jesus, the God-Man. It needs no deep consideration to work up the difficult practice of virtue. To transform itself wholly into Jesus is the one thought that absorbs it and prepares it for any sacrifice.

What an ideal for a creature, to be changed into Jesus by such a transformation! The ideal captivates a generous soul and leads it to perfection. A priest, especially, is called to a life of identification with Christ. Are not the Mass, administration of the sacraments, liturgical prayers, the essence of a life lived in Christ's name? Should he not aspire to conform his interior to his exterior life? A general complaint arises that so few believers follow God seriously. It is worth asking if may be due to the idea of holiness presented to them.

Spirituality of a certain type seems to stop short, or nearly so, on the threshold of the unitive life. Granted, it has helped the soul purify itself, to acquire Christian virtue. It ought to go further, to take the soul out of itself, so as to live before all else a life of union. To teach that, it must also be taught to enjoy God. It must have some initiation into the life of union.

Unfortunately, these practices stop at the threshold of the unitive way. Too negative in character, they need something more positive, such as some very noble and sublime ideal. For lack of this ideal, many souls stop by degrees and end up standing still. If offered St. Paul's great ideal, even a glimpse of it, the most generous would stand a better chance of answering the call of holiness.

Preoccupation with self

One of the many traps in the spiritual life, even for those on the threshold of holiness, is over-concern with oneself. Whether thinking too much about themselves, analyzing their feelings minutely, or reproaching themselves excessively for failings and unfaithfulness, they fret too much about their spiritual progress. Undoubtedly this comes from their zeal, as well as their love for God, but this love is not free enough from self-love. How much they would gain by thinking less of self and more of God! They should apply to themselves the words of our Lord to St. Margaret Mary: "Forget yourself entirely and I will think of you." The soul which seeks to live the life of Christ learns to forget itself. At every moment it sees things from God's standpoint. It forgets individual interests and aims, to embrace the wider interests of Christ. No place exists for excessive anxiety over the soul. With eyes fixed on Christ, it does not look at itself.

This attitude is infinitely valuable, especially for those souls whom God fills with special graces. These souls are often tempted to turn their eyes on themselves, even while scarcely aware of doing so, and to draw satisfaction from the gifts they have received.

Also note how such spirituality influences mystic life and mystic prayer. The development of the spiritual life, as a rule, presupposes the highest degree of mystical graces, making up the spiritual marriage or transforming union which is the climax of Christian perfection. If the soul is one with Christ, this favors the unitive life by filling the soul with the right sentiments and ideas. This influence is better understood if we consider that the mystical life's development implies both passivity and docility to the Holy Spirit.

Mystical life and mystical prayer tend to give greater emphasis to God's influence in the soul, whether for contemplation or action. God's influence makes itself felt in an infused and ever more perceptible manner, while the soul becomes more and more passive. God becomes the chief protagonist of the soul's actions, while soul's response lies in following these promptings. God transforms the soul by substituting his life and action through these promptings, internal "lights" or understandings. He wishes to become everything to the soul, to be its only master, and therefore he bestows ever more precious mystic graces. Thanks to these, his life and his action are perceived by the soul in an ever more penetrating degree.

This plan of God is exactly what the soul seeks if it wants to become identified with Christ. It aims at decreasing, or losing itself, at simply becoming an instrument of Christ. "He must increase, but I must decrease" (Jn 3:30). The soul's ideal becomes "It is no longer I who live, but Christ who lives in me" (Gal 2:20). What can do more to favor the growth of mystical life and prayer? To what heights will that soul reach, when every aspiration, ideal and effort blends with the aim pursued unceasingly by God?

Such a soul wastes no time pursuing one or other virtue of its choice, or in desiring things that are not part of God's plan. It stays detached from consolations or gifts of God. Its whole spiritual life is attentive and docile to God's action, in following all his inspirations, so that it may be nothing, and Christ everything. The favorite virtue is neither humility or mortification, nor anything, but one that includes all others—a loving docility to the heart's guest. The expression "a loving docility" accurately sums up the soul's efforts, and calls to mind the gifts of the Holy Spirit. In this way, the spiritual way favors the development and influence of these gifts. They render the soul ever more obediently loving and more lovingly obedient to the gentlest of divine inspirations.

Thus, the efforts of God and of the soul tend in the same direction. The mystic action of God coincides perfectly with the action of the soul.

No effort goes to waste in the pursuit of perfection since there are no useless advances in the wrong direction. Nothing is lost. The words of St. Paul are completely verified in this regard, "We know that in everything God works for good with those who love him" (Rom 8:28).

From a psychological point of view, this spirituality and the mystical life necessarily influence each other. The soul that seeks unceasingly to live Jesus's life, rather than its own, better recognizes the mystic and least perceptible touches of this life within itself. With all its attention concentrated on the life of Jesus, the experience of this sense of life and action of Jesus will be noticed. That soul becomes inflamed with love and welcomes these free gifts of God. On the other hand, the passive sense of the life of Jesus within influences the spiritual life and renders it more faithful to transformation. This is the Pauline identification with Christ, "I live, now not I . . ."

The Prayer of Quiet

This passive experience supposes a certain degree of mystic life or prayer. In the ordinary prayer of quiet, the soul feels the divine presence within or near. It hardly feels Jesus acting and living within. It is not yet conscious that the infused love, which delights or transports, is the love of Jesus living within. Such a grace belongs to a higher degree, especially after a "dark night of the soul" when it feels invaded by the life of Jesus and his transforming action within. The soul perceives this action in the higher forms of the prayer of quiet, but this is of little consequence. What's important is that mystic graces render the soul still more faithful and more generous in pursuing to the end its ideal of transformation into Christ.

How does this happen? These graces make it more fully alive to the life of Jesus within. They are a confirmation of the spirituality that the soul adopts. The soul thrills with happiness in feeling the beat of Jesus's heart within, knowing that it is Jesus who set that heart on fire with love for his heavenly father. This thought intoxicates it with a joy that longs for the desire to fulfill even the smallest wish of its divine friend.

A soul which ardently desires to be transformed and obeys the divine impulses can count on God filling it with even greater graces. Forebodings of difficulties only strengthen, by contrast, the consciousness of Jesus. Step by step through the dark night, the soul arrives, if God so wills, at the divine espousals and spiritual marriage.

Passive purification

The great trial of passive purification, by means of which God works in the soul's very depths, prepares the soul for the supreme ascent and final transformation. This terrible trial is a veritable purgatory here below, according to St. John of the Cross. Spiritual directors generally feel powerless to comfort the soul in this phase of the spiritual life. God hammers, chisels, and sculpts as he will. Since he alone inflicts the wounds, only he can cure them.

The soul which is firmly rooted in the confidence of God's life in it has the best chance of passing through this period without being upset and discouraged. The heart-piercing vision of miseries, inactivity and complete helplessness assumes at times a frightening aspect: hitherto unknown temptations assail it. Despite this fury, the soul sees, in the flood of a secret and blinding light of infused contemplation, the dazzling holiness of God and its own deep-rooted sinfulness and deformity. Tormented by acute sufferings of love, it undergoes the strange torture of being deeply loved by God yet thinking itself empty of love. A life which is intended to please God, pines, and withers away under the obsession that it is too wicked and ugly to please him, and that God no longer loves it. This soul perhaps feels itself drowning in despair, unless it has a secret hope, or at least a glimmer of confidence. It tells itself that Jesus remains faithful in spite of all its miseries and faults, whether known or hidden.

Jesus remains the anchor of salvation in a furious storm. Surely that divine friend, who formerly made the soul feel its delightful presence and loving words, could not and never has abandoned it. He who identified himself and to whom the soul turned, who asked for a faithful love, who sought promises of absolute fidelity, could not desert, or abandon it. Though its hope disappears, though it remains only with a vague and bitter remembrance of past graces, yet it still recalls what Jesus insisted on: confidence. Before this storm began, had he not always demanded an absolute and blind confidence, despite all contrary appearances, a confidence not based on merit but on his goodness and faithfulness? Thus, Jesus secretly hints at the coming storm. So the tormented soul cannot, and will not, believe in its heart that Jesus has left it to its fate.

A sea of doubts and anguish may assault it. It suffers at certain times the sorrow of being abandoned, justly so, by the heavenly Father. It believes that Jesus has not abandoned it and is only hiding. The sufferer does not dare lift its eyes to the Father. In bitterness it strikes its breast in the presence of the infinite being whose holiness terrifies. But it has not the same fear of Jesus. This very friend of every moment, who was always beside it, as both mediator and assistant, does not and cannot assume a terrifying aspect.

No, the soul has no fear of Jesus. It still believes, unconsciously and instinctively, in his goodness and his love. But what anguish not to find Jesus, who could save, console, and reassure. Where is Jesus? Where is the beloved one? Like the spouse in the Song of Solomon, the soul rises in vain in the night to seek for him. "Upon my bed by night I sought him whom my soul loves; I sought him but found him not" (Song 3:1). Quivering with anguish and with loud cries, it calls out from its deepest recesses. In the darkness it still sends its bitter love, and secretly hopes in his mediation and restoration.

And thus, it clings desperately to Jesus as a shipwrecked sailor clings to a rock. It may resist for years all the storm's assaults until it ends. The dawn eventually comes, and it hears again the voice of its beloved: "Arise, my love, my fair one, and come away; for lo, the winter is past, the rain is over and gone" (Song 2:10).

CHAPTER FIVE

∽

Resolutions

TO DRAW SOME PRACTICAL RESOLUTIONS, the following list of suggestions includes some explanation. These resolutions all express the same idea that Christ may live and reign in us through all the circumstances of life. Each may choose what attracts them, or which they think they need. Remember that to give ourselves completely to the unitive life, a previous effort needs to be made both to root out faults and to struggle to acquire virtues.

1. Through sanctifying grace, Jesus is present in my soul, which serves him constantly as a living tabernacle. This devotion should complement the devotion to Jesus in the Blessed Sacrament. To recall this truth, and

to meditate it, the appropriate spiritual reading should become an essential part of daily life.

2. To build up my interior life and to put my conviction into daily practice by continual union with Jesus present within me. A spirit of interior recollection precedes a life of union with Jesus and initiation into the life of identification.

3. To realize through meditation, aspirations, and daily life that Jesus lives and acts in me. He demands my entire being so that through me he perpetuates his life of love on earth and continues to love his Father immensely.

4. In proportion to my understanding this great thought, I express it in the smallest details of my life. A constant thought occupies me, that of pleasing Jesus always, and yielding my life to him so that he may have his Father and his Blessed Mother as he pleases with an ever-purer love.

5. To allow Jesus to take complete possession of me, I try to be perfectly docile to his divine inspirations.

6. I never hesitate about any sacrifice, when I see that Jesus desires it. How could I wish to be myself rather than him?

7. I accustom myself to do nothing alone but everything in close union with Jesus. To go with him to prayer, good works, daily duties, dealings with my neighbor, and even the most indifferent actions.

8. To perform all actions through love, with the intention of pleasing Jesus. I look at this life of identification with Jesus as the most complete and loving donation I can make. No greater love exists than giving one's life for one's friend. In identifying with my savior, at every moment I give him my life.

9. I feed the flame of my love by the practice of loving aspirations. I frequently tell Jesus how sorry I am for forgetting him and instead live my own life.

10. I have great devotion to Jesus in the Blessed Sacrament and union with him in the Blessed Sacrament and in the Holy Eucharist. Fervent daily communion best increases the life of Jesus within me.

11. Through this life of identification, I surrender all joys to him. He is perfectly free to use me as he pleases, to satisfy all his divine desires and take to himself all my life's joys. I do not willingly allow any joy, desire, fear, or sadness that is personal or selfish.

12. To mortify myself as joyfully as possible, but always from the motive of love of Jesus, I shall grow to love mortification as the means of substituting my worthless self for the infinite perfections of Jesus. Thus, my purgative life overflows with unitive life.

13. I desire Jesus to have full liberty to live his life within my soul, which is encouraged to imitate his divine virtues. I give him constant joy in satisfying in me his longing for virtue, humility, charity, and thirst for souls.

14. I remind myself frequently that Jesus, who so loves the Cross, desires to satisfy in me his love of suffering. Thus, I will face sufferings joyfully, and bear them with courage.

15. Since Jesus is to live in me as he pleases, I must love God with him and as he does, with that very pure love which is proper to the unitive life. To begin, I must love God alone. Then, like Jesus, I will love God as my own possession.

16. I will forget myself to live in God, the love of my soul. I will foster thoughts and feelings calculated to develop the unitive life in me. I will meditate on the loveable perfections of God, of Jesus, and of his Blessed Mother, and do so frequently as the attraction grows.

17. I will try to fill my soul with a calm and deep happiness at the thought that God is infinitely perfect and happy.

18. I will frequently consider the infinite merits of Jesus to strengthen my soul in its joy

and perfect confidence. I will offer him the actions, prayers and sufferings through which Jesus glorifies his Father in me and with me. When guilty of an imperfection, I will offer to the Father the heart of Jesus, and in this love I will bury all my miseries.

19. I will try to become less selfish in my spiritual life, by looking at things from Jesus's standpoint. I will try to learn what he would feel if he stood in my place and substitute his feelings for mine. I will want my spiritual life to be full of wide and manifold interests, by adopting the interests of Jesus who lives in me.

20. If Jesus attracts me to a simpler, more peaceful method of prayer, I will not oppose his action in my soul.

21. I will apply the life of identification with Jesus to the life of my Mother Mary.

CHAPTER SIX

∞

Conclusion

Souls who struggle along the paths of perfection one day see a magnificent vista reveal itself. A deep change takes place in them, for some gradually and unknowingly, and for others, suddenly and in a marked way. Without being aware of the transformation, they find themselves regarding events through the eyes of Jesus, living his life and referring everything to him.

Life becomes a hymn of love which Jesus sings in and through them to the Father's glory. Their capacity to please God increases ten-fold. They delight that they are not alone in loving God, but Jesus loves in them. The infinite treasure of Jesus enriches their poverty.

What then, takes place? The Master's guidance leads them to make the spiritual life their ideal so that Jesus continues his life in them. Many long journeys with many false steps occurred before they reached where God had willed them to go. Not a few exclaim to themselves, "If I only understood God's plans, how much time I would not have wasted if I knew from the very start the ideal which now fills me with joy."

If the vision of a life identified with Christ and transformed by him was more clearly set before souls, how many generous hearts would more rapidly reach the highest level of the spiritual life?

Odd it is that an idea so characteristic of St. Paul should be so rare and ignored in practice. This conception of spiritual life in the seventeenth century played an important part in religious literature. The Jesuit mystics, led by Fr. Pierre Lallemant and his followers, drew on the presence of Jesus and the Holy Spirit in the soul. All spiritual life centered around guarding the

Conclusion

heart and being docile to the least impulses of the Holy Spirit, the spirit of Jesus, in order to permit him to live perfectly in us.

The teaching of St. John Eudes shows more clearly the ideas set forth in these pages. In his *Kingdom of Jesus* (*Works, volume 1*, 164), he says: "As St. Paul assures us that he fills us the sufferings of Christ, so we may say in truth that a true Christian . . . carries to completion, by every action performed in the spirit of Jesus Christ, the actions which Christ himself performed during the time of his peaceful life on earth."

This saint carries far the idea of identification with Christ: "In order to receive thee, not in myself being too unworthy of this, but in thee and with the love thou bears, I annihilate at thy feet my whole being . . . so that when coming to me in Holy Communion, thou mayest be received, not in me, but in thyself." (*Works*, *volume 1*, 140–141).

If this sublime doctrine were better known, souls who now vegetate in a state of mediocrity would soon rise to great heights of union. Only through the Holy Spirit do many come to a life of union and transformation, without knowing exactly where they are going. If these souls were clearly instructed, then those whom God leads by the way of passive contemplation would become far more numerous.

In order to truly identify with Jesus, souls need to reproduce all of his states and virtues. For an entire life to be one of self-denial and sacrifice, it must relive the sufferings and passion of Christ. It is none the less true that for most souls, Jesus fulfills in them one or other state of his mortal life. All are called to put on Jesus Christ, to be transformed into him. If they second God's action, it will not be long before they become other Christs.

A life of union and identification with Jesus should be based on the soul's consciousness of the real presence of Jesus (as the Divine Word) by sanctifying grace. Certain forms of spirituality claiming union with Jesus lose some or much value for holiness because they fail to dwell enough on the doctrine of the real presence. They create an impression of a union of pure fellowship, of friendship, or of complete donation of oneself. Even if they mention the presence of Jesus in us by his grace, it seems to suggest a presence by mere influence, rather than a real presence, and the created gift of grace rather than the divine indwelling.

CHAPTER SEVEN

Prayer to Unite with Jesus

O Jesus, my loving savior, you thirst for our souls to love within us, and through us, your heavenly Father, for whom you died on the Cross. You long for millions of lives and hearts to go on loving your Father until the end of time.

I come then, O Jesus, to give and consecrate myself entirely to you. May I be your possession, not belonging any more to myself, but completely to you, not existing any more for my own enjoyment but only for yours. Do in me and with me all you wish. Fully identified with you, may I become another soul who loves passionately your heavenly Father and Blessed Mother.

May my eyes become your eyes, that look only on what you wish to see. May my lips speak only your words, those of meekness, kindness, and loving charity. May my mind be filled with your divine thoughts. May my heart be dead with self-love, and instead glow with your ardent love for the Father and your untiring zeal for souls.

Help me, o divine master, to do everything with you and for you. Make me obedient to your divine inspirations, so that at each moment I may perfectly fulfill your desires. Help me to forget myself and fill me to the brim with you, so that like St. Paul I may not live but you alone live within me. Be the life of my soul and the soul of my life. May I desire only to express continually your love for the Father, and my one joy to be your joy, by giving you to God, to the Blessed Virgin Mary, and to souls, through my every act. Amen.